A TRUE BOOK

W9-AXE-625

Oceans

PETER BENOIT

Children's Press®
An Imprint of Scholastic Inc.
New York   Toronto   London   Auckland   Sydney
Mexico City   New Delhi   Hong Kong
Danbury, Connecticut

Content Consultant
David L. Taylor, PhD
Roger Williams University
Bristol, Rhode Island

Library of Congress Cataloging-in-Publication Data

Benoit, Peter, 1955–
  Oceans/Peter Benoit.
     p. cm.—(A true book)
  Includes bibliographical references and index.
  ISBN-13: 978-0-531-20556-3 (lib. bdg.)   978-0-531-28105-5 (pbk.)
  ISBN-10: 0-531-20556-8 (lib. bdg.)   0-531-28105-1 (pbk.)
  1. Oceanography—Juvenile literature. 2. Ocean—Juvenile literature. I. Title.
  GC21.5.B46 2011
  578.77—dc22   2010045963

All rights reserved. Published in 2011 by Children's Press, an imprint of Scholastic Inc.
Printed in USA. 08
SCHOLASTIC, CHILDREN'S PRESS, A TRUE BOOK and associated logos are trademarks and/or registered trademarks of Scholastic Inc.

 2 3 4 5 6 7 8 9 10 R 18 17 16 15 14 13 12

Duck!

On January 10, 1992, a ship in the North Pacific lost a dozen containers in a storm. One container held thousands of yellow rubber ducks and other plastic toys. Ten months later, a wave of the toys washed up in Alaska. In 1996, more appeared in Washington State. Others circled back to Japan. Some even drifted to New England and Europe. By tracking where the toys landed, scientists learned a lot about ocean circulation.

Curt Ebbesmeyer tracked the plastic toys as they washed up on shores around the world.

13

Bottlenose dolphins are
friendly and intelligent.

Ocean Life

The ocean is home to an astonishing variety of living things. The 230,000-plus known life-forms include sponges, shrimps, lobsters, squid, jellyfish, and more than 16,750 species of fish. Plankton and other tiny life-forms serve as vital food sources near the bottom of the oceanic food chain. Large mammals such as walruses, dolphins, and whales live near the top. Scientists believe a total of 2 million animal species may live in the oceans, though most are yet to be discovered.

 Studies suggest that dolphins recognize their own reflections in a mirror.

Habitats Large and Small

Each species is adapted to a **habitat** that meets its requirements to live and reproduce. Algae, for example, live in the photic zone because they need sunlight to live. This means animals that eat algae also need to live in the photic zone. Some ocean animals live along the coast. Others live out in open waters. Every habitat is filled with a variety of creatures that rely on one another to survive.

Pilot fish follow sharks, feeding on the scraps left when the sharks eat.

Coral reefs grow in the shallow waters of the sea shelf.

All About Coral

Coral are colorful sea animals with hard skeletons. These skeletons can be on the inside or the outside of the coral. They come in many shades and shapes, from red and tube-shaped to yellow and spiky. One end of each coral **polyp** attaches to rocks or the ocean floor. When coral die, they leave their skeletons behind. New polyps grow on the skeletons. This causes **coral reefs** to form.

Scientists estimate the Great Barrier Reef began forming half a million years ago.

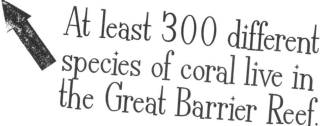

At least 300 different species of coral live in the Great Barrier Reef.

The Great Barrier Reef

Thousands of species of ocean life make coral reefs their home. These colorful ocean habitats are known as the rain forests of the sea. They are found in the shallow waters along coastlines. Australia's Great Barrier Reef is the largest of all. It is more than 1,250 miles (2,000 kilometers) long and made up of almost 3,000 smaller reefs.

Life in the Reef

Coral reefs are home to lobsters, crabs, and brightly colored fish. Sea horses, sponges, and anemones live there, too. The coral provides them with food and shelter. Some animals, such as the crown-of-thorns starfish, eat the coral. Others eat the algae that form on dead coral polyps. A bigger animal, such as an octopus, might feed on the smaller animals that swim and crawl around the reef.

A coral reef is home to animals of all shapes, sizes, and eating habits.

Sharks on the Hunt

More than 400 species of sharks live in Earth's oceans. Some are very small, such as the 8-inch (20-centimeter) deepwater dogfish shark. Others, like the 60-foot (18 m) whale shark, are gigantic. Even though whale sharks are huge, they only eat tiny plankton. Other sharks, such as the great white and the hammerhead, are dangerous hunters with sharp teeth. They eat seals, dolphins, and even other sharks.

Sharks sink if they stop swimming.

Orcas are often found in the cold waters of the northern Atlantic and Pacific oceans.

Other Ocean Hunters

The ocean is also home to many other large hunters. Bottlenose dolphins swim through the water at speeds of up to 18.5 miles per hour (30 km per hour). They hunt in groups, using sound waves to find small fish to eat. Orcas hunt larger animals such as seals and whales. Other animals, such as blue whales and manta rays, swim through the ocean with their mouths open to capture tiny animals.

A dragonfish

22

CHAPTER 3

Creatures of the Deep

The bottom of the ocean is totally dark. It is a completely different world compared to the zones closer to the surface. In 1960, Jacques Piccard and Don Walsh rode down to the bottom of the Mariana Trench in a submersible named the *Trieste*. The trip to the ocean floor took almost five hours. What they saw resembled another planet.

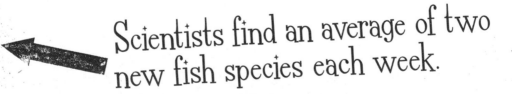

Scientists find an average of two new fish species each week.

Black Smokers

Giant tube worms live near **volcanic vents** called black smokers on the ocean floor, miles beneath the surface. It is a dark world of immense water pressure and heat. Water in the vents can often reach 765 degrees Fahrenheit (407 degrees Celsius) and sometimes spike to even higher temperatures. The vents flood the nearby seawater with sulfur. Bacteria on the worms change the sulfur into food for their worm hosts.

Giant tube worms

Species living in extreme habitats are called extremophiles.

When in danger, squid squirt ink into the water. The ink helps hide the squid so it can escape.

New Squid in Town

In 2004, researchers took the first photos of a giant squid in its deep-ocean habitat. It turned out that giant squid females can reach lengths of 43 feet (13 m) and weigh more than 600 pounds (270 kg). Males are smaller. A giant squid's eight arms and two long tentacles are lined with tiny suction cups. Razor-sharp teeth surround each cup. Sperm whales, the giant squid's main predator, often have scars from the cups.

Glowing Seas

At night, the ocean's blue-green glow is visible for miles. This is caused by **bioluminescence** (by-oh-loo-muh-NEH-sints) — light produced by living

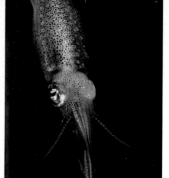

Market squids are usually about 11 inches (30 cm) long.

organisms. Scientists believe that up to 90 percent of deep-sea animals may use bioluminescence to hunt, hide, or find mates, or for other reasons. These animals range from tiny shrimplike krill to many squid species and the cookie-cutter shark.

Timeline of Ocean Discovery

1513
Sailors discover the Gulf Stream, a massive warm current.

1960
The *Trieste* dives 36,201 feet (11,034 m) to the bottom of the ocean.

The Bioluminescent Future

Bioluminescence may be useful to humans. Scientists think it may be possible one day to create bioluminescent crops that glow when they need to be watered. Bioluminescent trees along highways, meanwhile, could eliminate the need for expensive electric lights. Even pets such as rabbits and mice could be engineered into breeds that glow.

1977
Black smokers, or volcanic vents, are discovered.

1986
Alvin **takes scientists to the** *Titanic* **wreck.**

2004
The first giant squid photos are taken.

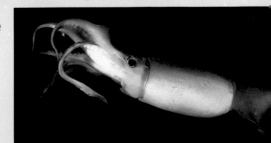

Deep-Ocean Vehicles

Only special vehicles called submersibles can make it to the deepest parts of the ocean. Submersibles are small submarines built of superstrong metals such as titanium. This metal can withstand cold as well as high water pressure. Submersibles are equipped with video cameras, powerful lights, and robotic arms with claws that can grab objects. Usually, they hold one to three passengers.

Find the Truth!

Everything you are about to read is true *except* for one of the sentences on this page.

Which one is **TRUE**?

T or F A garbage patch the size of the United States is floating in the Pacific Ocean.

T or F Palm trees do not grow on the coast of Scotland.

Find the answers in this book.

Contents

THE **BIG** TRUTH!

A dragonfish

The *Alvin* submersible has been diving since 1964.

4 A World in Motion

In what ways does the ocean move?

5 A Force to Be Reckoned With

How does the ocean help to regulate climate?

Walruses basking in the sun

5

Kayakers explore the Pacific waters off the coast of Mexico.

CHAPTER 1

Many Worlds in One

The ocean is its own world. Water flows freely around continents and through straits and canals from one part of the globe to another. All Earth's oceans are connected and share certain traits. For example, ocean water has 3.5 percent **salinity**. That means for every 100 pounds (45.4 kilograms) of water there are about 3.5 pounds (1.6 kg) of salt.

 The Pacific is the world's largest ocean.

Oceans by the Numbers

Oceans cover almost 71 percent of Earth's surface. The water in more than half of it is deeper than 9,800 feet (3,000 meters). The deepest point scientists have discovered is 36,200 feet (11,034 m) below the surface in the Mariana Trench in the western Pacific Ocean. If Mount Everest, the world's tallest mountain, were placed inside the trench, its top would still be under almost 7,165 feet (2,184 m) of water.

Seventeen of Earth's 20 major trenches are located in the Pacific Ocean basin.

The Mariana Trench is located to the east of the Mariana Islands.

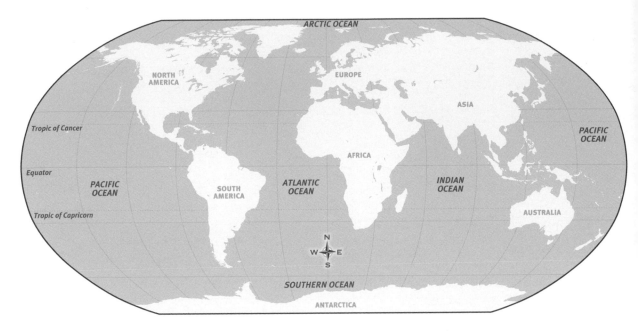

This map shows Earth's oceans.

Bodies of Water

Five vast areas of water, each referred to as an
ocean, make up the larger world ocean. They are
the Pacific, Atlantic, Indian, Southern, and Arctic.
Smaller regions of oceans go by names such as seas,
gulfs, bays, channels, and straits. As important as
these divisions are to sailors and scientists alike,
the labels only begin to tell the story.

The sea shelf can extend miles from shore, though it is often too deep to wade across.

The Lighted Ocean

Scientists divide the ocean into zones based on depth, temperature, and the amount of light available in the water. The coastal waters, for example, are called the neritic (nur-IT-ik) zone. Most people who visit the seashore have waded in the neritic zone. It extends over the seafloor, or shelf, that hangs off dry land. Because the shelf is not far down, neritic zone waters tend to be shallow.

The seafloor takes a steep plunge at the edge of the shelf. The open ocean takes over. Experts call the area from the water's surface to the point where no light can pass through the water the **photic zone**. The photic zone usually ranges from 330 to 660 feet (100 to 200 m) deep. Most ocean life-forms live part or all of the time in the photic zone. The many forms of animals and plants give the photic layer the greatest **biodiversity** of any ocean zone.

Plants require sunlight and grow only in the photic zone.

Into the Deep

The aphotic (ay-FOH-tick) layer lies beneath the thin photic layer. It has three zones. The first is the middle pelagic (puh-LA-jick), or twilight, zone. Next is the bathyal (bath-EE-uhl), or midnight, zone. Even deeper is the abyssal (uh-BIS-uhl) zone, also called the **abyss**. Below the abyss lies the hadal (HAY-duhl) zone, which extends to the bottom of the deepest ocean trenches. Life that exists in these zones gets energy from sources other than sunlight.

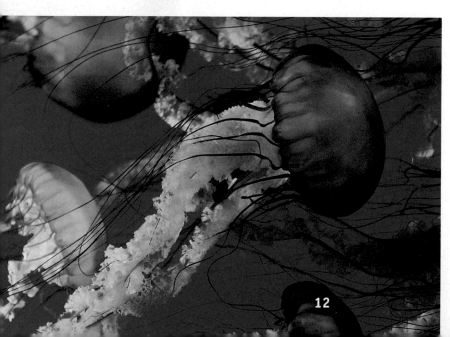

Jellyfish can be found in every layer of the ocean.

Alvin: Submersible Legend

In service since 1964, *Alvin* discovered black smokers and later explored the *Titanic* wreck.

Mir 1 and 2: Twin Ships

The three-person Russian *Mir 1* vehicle planted a metal Russian flag 13,979 feet (4,261 m) under the North Pole.

In 1960, the *Trieste* carried two explorers to the Challenger Deep, the lowest point on Earth.

CHAPTER 4

A World in Motion

The ocean is never at rest. Its waves, tides, and currents shape coastlines and influence wildlife. They also have a powerful effect on Earth's climate.

Waves result from winds blowing over the ocean surface. Faster winds mean bigger waves. Other factors such as how long the wind has blown and water depth also play a part in the formation of waves.

 Surfing is an ancient sport among Pacific Island peoples.

Ocean Movement

Wind and gravity act with salinity and temperature differences to produce currents. A current is a movement of water in a certain direction.

In each **hemisphere**, or half of Earth, winds blow both from east to west and from west to east depending on **latitude**. These winds work with other factors to produce surface currents that affect the top layers of the ocean.

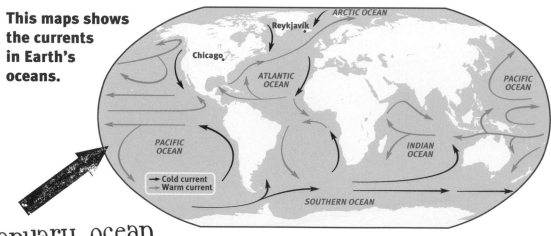

This maps shows the currents in Earth's oceans.

In January, ocean currents keep Reykjavik, Iceland, warmer than Chicago, Illinois.

Currents and Climate

Currents play an important role in climate. The Gulf Stream is one of the best-known examples. It is a massive warm current that starts off the coast of North Carolina and follows the eastern coastline of the United States and Canada. It splits as it crosses the Atlantic Ocean. The northern branch of the current brings weather that warms northern Europe. Gulf Stream warming even encourages palm trees to grow on Scotland's western coast.

Palm trees growing on the Isle of Arran in Scotland

Debris from the Great Pacific Garbage Patch sometimes washes up on beaches.

Garbage, Garbage Everywhere

Bound by four major ocean currents, the waters of the North Pacific **Gyre** rotate slowly. In recent years, the area has become an enormous garbage patch. It is choked with plastic, chemicals, and waste. Currents and winds in coastal waters pick up the material from Japan, China, North America, and elsewhere. Once it reaches the gyre dead zone, it just sits there.

It's been named the Great Pacific Garbage Patch, and it is mostly invisible. Nature has broken down the plastic into tiny bits. But it may still threaten human health by adding garbage to the food chain. What happens? Small sea creatures eat the plastic. Fish, in turn, eat the creatures. Humans may then absorb the plastic by eating the fish. It is possible the plastic contains dangerous chemicals. This makes a bad situation worse.

Samples are taken from the garbage patch to test for chemicals and to show the effects of pollution.

The Atlantic Ocean also has a garbage patch.

The Greenhouse Effect

The ocean stores enormous amounts of a gas called carbon dioxide. That's a good thing, because too much carbon dioxide in the atmosphere increases temperatures by adding to what's called the greenhouse effect. A greenhouse effect occurs when layers of gases trap the sun's heat near the surface of Earth. Because carbon dioxide contributes to the greenhouse effect, it's called a greenhouse gas.

Too much carbon dioxide in the atmosphere traps heat from the sun near Earth's surface.

Sun

Heat that escapes Earth's atmosphere

Heat trapped near Earth's surface

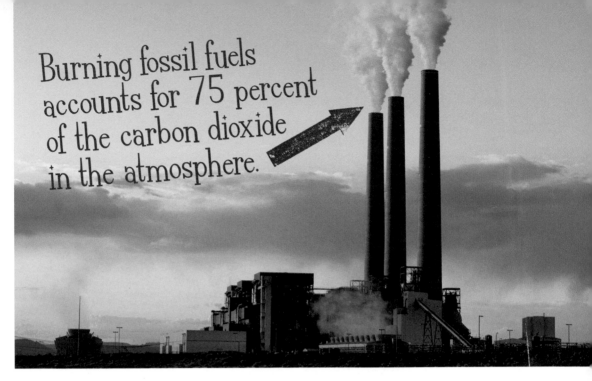

Burning fossil fuels accounts for 75 percent of the carbon dioxide in the atmosphere.

The world's power plants are a major source of carbon dioxide in Earth's atmosphere.

Much of our electricity and fuel comes from burning fossil fuels such as coal, petroleum (oil), and natural gas. When burned, all add carbon dioxide to the atmosphere, as do burning forests. Nature can no longer keep up with this increase in greenhouse gases. The melting Arctic ice and warmer temperatures in southern Europe are two signs of this.

Ocean Energy Source

Scientists and engineers think the ocean may provide one alternative to fossil fuels. Today, they are looking into how to build fields of electricity-generating **turbines** about 1,000 feet (300 m) underwater, off the Florida coast. Florida is an excellent place to test the turbines because areas of its coast sit just 15 miles (24 km) from the powerful Gulf Stream.

A 30,000 pounds (13,600 kg) weight would anchor each turbine.

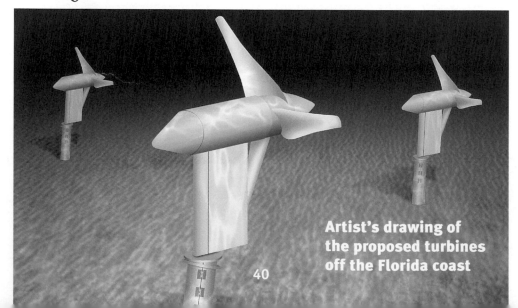

Artist's drawing of the proposed turbines off the Florida coast

Sea-powered electricity would help much of Florida become more eco-friendly.

The turbines look like underwater windmills, with blades 100 feet (30 m) in diameter. Once placed in the Gulf Stream, the turbines would convert the energy of moving water to electrical power. A field of turbines, if built, might one day provide electricity for one-third of Florida. Using sea power would allow Floridians to reduce the amount of fossil fuels burned to generate electricity.

The Future for Earth's Oceans

In many ways, our future depends on our better understanding the resources and delicate nature of the ocean ecosystem. The ocean affects our lives every moment of every day, even the lives of those who live far from its waters. It is both a source of food and an influence on climate. Scientists tell us the world ocean may hold the secret of the origin of life on Earth. It will play a key role in life's survival, too. ★

Ocean coasts are some of the most populated areas in the world.

True Statistics

Amount of seawater that is salt: 3.5 percent

Amount of Earth covered by oceans: 71 percent

Average ocean depth: 12,450 ft. (3,795 m)

Depth of Mariana Trench: 36,200 ft. (11,034 m)

Depth of the photic zone: 660 ft. (200 m)

Plastic added to oceans per year: 20 billion lbs. (9 billion kg)

Average January high, Chicago, Illinois: 32°F (0°C)

Average January high, Reykjavik, Iceland: 35°F (2°C)

Number of known ocean life-forms: More than 230,000

Length of female giant squid: 43 ft. (13 m)

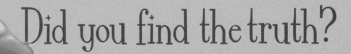

Did you find the truth?

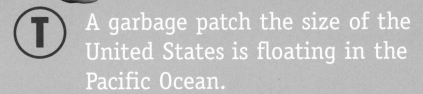

(T) A garbage patch the size of the United States is floating in the Pacific Ocean.

(F) Palm trees do not grow on the coast of Scotland.

Resources

Books

Berger, Melvin. *What Makes an Ocean Wave?* New York: Scholastic Reference, 2001.

Champion, Neil. *Seas and Oceans*. North Mankato, MN: Smart Apple Media, 2007.

Ganeri, Anita. *Oceans in Danger*. Danbury, CT: Children's Press, 2006.

Green, Emily K. *Oceans*. New York: Children's Press, 2006.

Hall, Kirsten. *Deep Sea Adventures: A Chapter Book*. New York: Children's Press, 2003.

Mason, Paul. *Ocean in Motion*. Mankato, MN: Capstone Press, 2008.

Parker, Jane. *Oceans*. Brookfield, CT: Copper Beach Books, 1999.

Sexton, Colleen. *Squid*. Minneapolis: Bellwether Media, 2008.

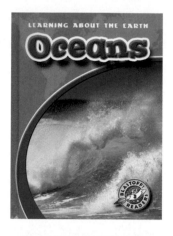

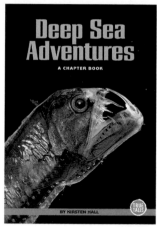

Organizations and Web Sites

NASA: In Search of Giant Squid
http://seawifs.gsfc.nasa.gov/squid.html
Explore articles and pictures of the mysterious sea giants in an online exhibit.

Office of Naval Research—Oceanography
www.onr.navy.mil/focus/ocean/
Read student-oriented articles on all aspects of ocean life.

Woods Hole Oceanographic Institution: For Students
www.whoi.edu/page.do?pid=9544
Ocean scientists offer videos and articles on many subjects.

Places to Visit

Monterey Bay Aquarium
886 Cannery Row
Monterey, California 93940
(831) 648-4800
www.montereybay
aquarium.org
One of the world's great aquariums.

Shedd Aquarium
1200 S. Lake Shore Drive
Chicago, IL 60605
(312) 939-2438
www.sheddaquarium.org
The Shedd Aquarium is famous as a home for beluga whales.

Important Words

abyss (uh-BISS) — a very deep part of the ocean

biodiversity (BY-oh-de-VERS-sih-tee) — the number of different life-forms in an ecosystem

bioluminescence (by-oh-loo-muh-NEH-sints) — the light created by a living organism

coral reefs (KOR-uhl REEFS) — shallow-water habitats made up of large groups of coral

gyre (JI-ur) — a large system of rotating ocean currents

habitat (HAB-uh-tat) — where an organism lives and grows

hemisphere (HEM-uhss-fihr) — half of Earth

latitude (LAT-uh-tood) — the distance from Earth's equator measured in degrees from 0 to 90.

photic zone (FOH-tik ZOHN) — the part of the ocean where light is still able to shine through the water

polyp (PAH-lip) — the body of a coral

salinity (suh-LIN-uh-tee) — the amount of salt dissolved in water

turbines (TER-bynz) — engines that take energy from water or wind and turn it into electricity

volcanic vents (val-KA-nik VENTS) — holes in the ocean floor where heat and minerals spill out

Index

Page numbers in **bold** indicate illustrations

About the Author

Peter Benoit is educated as a mathematician but has many other interests. He has taught and tutored high school and college students for many years, mostly in math and science. He also runs summer workshops for writers and students of literature. Mr. Benoit has also written more than 2,000 poems. His life has been one committed to learning. He lives in Greenwich, New York.